MW01264846

That's Great Advice

Advice from Pro Athletes for Kids, Written by a Kid

Matthew Pearlman

Follow your dreams!

MP

Published by FastPencil

Copyright © 2012 Matthew Pearlman

Published by FastPencil
3131 Bascom Ave.
Suite 150
Campbell CA 95008 USA
info@fastpencil.com
(408) 540-7571
(408) 540-7572 (Fax)
http://www.fastpencil.com

First Edition

This book is dedicated to all the kids and teens out there who are working hard each day to pursue their dreams.

❧

Acknowledgments

The athletes that I interviewed are very busy. I could not have completed this book without their time, support, open conversation, and kindness. Thank you to everyone who is featured in this book and to everyone else that has assisted in making this dream come true!

Thank you to my parents who have encouraged me to live my dream!

Thank you to my twin sister Samantha who has been there every step of the way!

Thank you to Amy Sterling Casil who helped me to organize my thoughts!

Thank you to Veronika Kucherov for designing the cover and to John Salangsang and the Harlem Globetrotters for the cover photo!

Thank you to Bruce Butterfield for helping guide us through the publishing process!

Thank you to Scott Norton, sports agent, who helped me with several of my first interviews! My dream job is to work with him after college.

Thank you to Tim Ezell (Fox 2 News & Neighborhood Basketball Association) for interviewing me on TV for the first time when I was 11. His advice and humor helped me to realize that I could do it!

Thank you to Grandma Phyllis for helping to edit this book!

Contents

Introduction

When I got the idea to interview pro athletes, nobody thought that an 11 year old would be taken seriously. After all, most sports journalists have years of experience covering games and interviewing athletes.

I also knew that anything worth having is worth fighting for. I decided that reaching my goal was so much better when getting there wasn't easy.

My mom and dad told me that I have been a fighter since I was born. My twin sister Samantha and I were born 9 weeks early and the two of us together only weighed about 6 pounds. We started our lives in the Neo-Natal Intensive Care Unit of St. John's Mercy Hospital in St. Louis. We were in an incubator for 6 weeks. My mom said that she knew we were fighters when we arrived home healthy and happy and 3 weeks before our actual due date. I guess we both got ahead of the game as babies.

When I started school, it definitely was not easy for me. Reading and writing were very difficult for me in Kindergarten through third grade. It was very frustrating and I felt like I would never be able to read or write well. With a lot of help, hard work, and determination, it became easier. A big part of my reading success came after I read sports biographies of Jackie Robinson, Shoeless Joe Jackson, Wayne Gretzky, Muhammad Ali, and Michael Jordan. These were very interesting and inspired me to read, research, and write papers about them.

When I decided to be a sports journalist, I worked hard to find out how to reach athletes. I made calls, faxed requests, mailed letters, and e-mailed many people. I was a little discouraged at first and wasn't sure if I would ever get any real interviews. I decided that I would keep working hard anyway, and I prepared interview notes and practiced mock interviews with my family. I wanted to be as professional as I could. This went on for a couple of months, but no one called back.

In June 2010, I was at home watching a St. Louis Cardinals game. The phone rang and the caller ID said BRETT HULL. He was one of the biggest stars with the St. Louis Blues hockey team and is in the NHL Hall of Fame. Brett Hull was one of the best goal scorers of all time. I almost fell over and couldn't believe it was really him. It turned out to be a great interview with an amazing player. I realized I had reached my goal.

Brett Hull has another connection to me that my dad told me about after the interview. On the day after I was born, my dad met Brett Hull in the elevator at St. John's Mercy Hospital. It turns out that Brett Hull's son was born on the same day in the same hospital as I was. I started to realize we all have more in common than we might think, from sports stars to kids who love sports.

I posted my interview with Brett Hull on my website **TeensOnSports.com** [http://www.teensonsports.com]. I have conducted over 500 more interviews since then.

When I got the idea for this book, I didn't know if kids would want to read it. The athletes had already given me a lot of advice, so I asked them if they would have read a book like this when they were in school. They all responded very positively. Their responses are located at the end of this book.

CHAPTER 1

Perseverance

Perseverance (noun): The continued effort to do or achieve something despite difficulties, failure, or opposition.

It's not so important who starts the game but who finishes it.
-UCLA Coach John Wooden

If I had to select one quality, one personal characteristic that I regard as being most highly correlated with success, whatever the field, I would pick the trait of persistence. The will to endure to the end, to get knocked down seventy times and get up off the floor saying. "Here comes number seventy-one!" -Founder of Amway Corporation Richard M. Devos

When I started interviewing pro athletes, I already knew they had to spend a lot of time practicing to be good at their sport or game. I knew that sometimes they had setbacks and had to keep trying in order to succeed. I also knew that athletes had injuries, and often had to work hard to recover, get strong again, and get back in the game.

Following through, sticking to the job, and finishing what you start are ways people talk about perseverance. After I interviewed the athletes, I learned that perseverance counts on the field and off. Sometimes things happen off the field that can affect your game. Sometimes it's the other way around. I learned that being an athlete can help other aspects of life too, like getting better grades or getting along with your friends and family.

Here are the athletes and their messages for kids about perseverance:

Cole Hamels (MLB)

Cole Hamels (credit - Dawn Shields)

Cole Hamels was born in December, 1983 in San Diego, California. He is one of Major League Baseball's top pitchers and is part of the starting lineup for the Philadelphia Phillies.

Cole has played baseball since he was four years old, and showed his talent in Little League. When he was in high school at Rancho Bernardo High School near San Diego, his 94 MPH fastball caught the eye of many MLB scouts. Cole's baseball future looked bright, but when he was sixteen, he broke his arm, and scouts lost interest.

Cole fought back from the injury and when he graduated from high school in 2002 was picked in the first round of the MLB draft by the Philadelphia Phillies. Cole received the Paul Owens Award as the best minor league pitcher for the Phillies in 2003, but in 2004 and 2005, Cole again suffered several injuries and missed a lot of baseball. In 2006, Cole returned to minor league baseball healthy and strong, and was called up to the majors in May, 2006. By the next year, Cole was named to the NL All Star team, finishing the season with a 15-5 record. The next year, 2008, was a great year for Cole and the Phillies. The Phillies won the NLCS and the World Series. Cole was not only named MVP for both post-season series, he also led the Phillies' World Series Victory parade. Cole returned to the World Series the next year and continues to stand out in the Phillies pitching lineup. Cole is married, and has two children with his wife Heidi. In addition to his MLB career, Heidi and Cole have their own foundation that raises money to support children's education around the world in order to fight poverty. They have supported schools in Philadelphia, and provide funding for an entire school for 2,700 children in Malawi, Africa.

Cole's advice for kids about perseverance:

"I broke my arm throwing a baseball when I was 16 and the doctor said I had a 1% chance of ever pitching again. I healed, got stronger and I achieved my goal of pitching in the major leagues. My message about perseverance is in order to succeed, you must learn from your failures and keep doing your best. Never give up on the game, and enjoy every moment you get playing baseball or any other sport."

Juan Pablo Montoya (NASCAR Driver)

Juan Pablo Montoya (credit – Action Sports Photography)

Starting from a young age, Juan Pablo Montoya was the fastest on the track no matter what he raced. The American NASCAR series star was a top Formula 1 racer in the world's fastest cars, driving for the world's top teams: BMW Williams and McLaren Mercedes. Juan Pablo won seven F-1 races, finished in the top three 30 times, and took 13 pole positions. In 2003, he won the prestigious Monaco Grand Prix. In Indy cars, Juan Pablo won the CART racing series in 1999, and made another huge impression when he won the 2000 Indianapolis 500 on his first time at the famous "Brickyard." He led a dominant 167 out of 200 laps around the track, a record for a rookie at the track.

Juan Pablo is the first Formula 1 driver to switch to racing full time in America's NASCAR racing series. He is the only driver to win the Indianapolis 500 and the 24 Hours of Daytona in the first attempt. Only one other driver, classic British driver Graham Hill, has also won the Indy 500 and the Monaco GP. Only Mario Andretti has equaled Juan Pablo's achievement of winning the Indy 500, an F-1 race, and a NASCAR championship race.

Growing up in Colombia, his father Pablo taught him the basics of racing and helped him get started by racing go-karts, the traditional start for open-wheel racecar drivers worldwide. He was the Colombian National Karting Champion from 1981 to 1984 — starting when he was 6 years old! By the time he was 17, he was winning more advanced Formula Renault races. He moved to Austria to race larger Formula 3000 cars, and with very little money, he couldn't even afford a bus or train to get to the track so he rollerbladed everywhere he wanted to go.

Together with his wife Connie, Juan Pablo created the Formula Smile Foundation, which is one of the most active racing charities building sports facilities for children in poor neighborhoods worldwide. He is also a United Nations Goodwill Ambassador.

Juan Pablo has lots of natural talent, but he told me that without perseverance, he would not be where he is today.

"Things were really tough for me in 1998 when I was living in Austria and looking for my big break in racing and had no money for anything. I used to rollerblade everywhere. You definitely have to have a lot of dedication and love for your sport to succeed. Racing is a tough sport and you're up against some of the best drivers in the world. But I'm now living my dream and can't imagine doing anything else."

Usain Bolt (Olympic Sprinter)

The world's fastest runner, Usain Bolt, is popular all over the world and is universally admired in his country - Jamaica. He is a five-time World Champion and three-time Olympic gold medalist and world record holder in the 100 meter and 200 meter races, and 4 x 100 meter relay. Usain's world record pace in the 100 meter race is 9.52 seconds. In 2011, Usain Bolt was named the World Male Athlete of the year for the third time. He is only the second athlete in history to receive this honor three different times.

Usain was born in August, 1986 in Trelawny, Jamaica, where he grew up with his brother Sadeeki and sister Sherine. His parents ran the local grocery store and Usain spent most of his time playing cricket and soccer with his brother. Usain said, "When I was young, I didn't really think about anything other than sports." At age 12, Usain was his school's fastest runner in the 100 meter race. His athletic talent earned him training opportunities and the chance to move to Kingston, Jamaica's capital city.

In 2002, Usain became the youngest participant to win the World Junior Championship in running. His biggest challenge came in 2004, when he injured his hamstring while training to defend his World Junior track and field championship. Recovering from his injury and learning perseverance led to the outstanding career Usain has had since.

In person, Usain is laid-back, loves music, and enjoys watching other sports like soccer and cricket. Usain is currently writing his autobiography.

Usain's message for kids about perseverance is:

"In 2004, I was injured and missed defending my World Junior title. I went to the Olympics that year but was unable to run properly due to the injury – this was the time I had to persevere. The best advice is something my coach Glen Mills told me – You have to learn to lose in order to learn to win."

Andre Dawson (MLB Hall of Famer)

"No player in baseball history worked harder, suffered more or did it better than Andre Dawson. He's the best I've ever seen. I watched him win an MVP for a last-place team in 1987, and it was the most unbelievable thing I've ever seen in baseball. He did it the right way, the natural way, and he did it in the field and on the bases and in every way."

Ryne Sandberg, Andre Dawson's teammate on the Chicago Cubs in 1987

Andre Dawson was born July 10, 1954 in Miami, Florida. Andre's nickname is "The Hawk," which he got when he was 10 years old. Following his dream of playing major league baseball, Andre he worked out with a men's baseball team that would hit him ground balls at practice. He tried as hard as he could to jump on the fast grounders. Watching him field the balls, his uncle said that most kids would shy away from a ball going that fast, but Andre attacked the ball "like a hawk."

During his 21-year Major League Baseball career, Andre batted .300 five times, drove in 100 runs four times, and had 13 seasons of 20 home runs. Andre is one of only three MLB players with 400 career home runs and 300 career stolen bases. The other players at this level are Willie Mays and Barry Bonds. Andre achieved all of this even though playing on the artificial turf at Montreal's Olympic Stadium damaged his knees, an injury that continued for the rest of his two-decade MLB career.

Andre's message about perseverance to kids is:

"I persevered through 20 years of playing Major League Baseball with bad knees. I worked hard every day on my knees. Sometimes it was difficult, but with a lot of help from trainers and doctors, I was able to play 21 MLB seasons."

Nikki Stone (Olympic Aerial Freestyle Skier)

When Nikki Stone was ten, she wasn't an aerial freestyle skiing champion, she was into gymnastics. She was good at it, too. By the time she was ten, she was competing in the state championship qualifier. After only three events, she found herself in first place. All she had to do was stick her balance beam routine so she would win.

Three-quarters of her way through her balance bar routine, Nikki slipped and fell. She saw her coach holding his head in his hands. Nikki got back up and finished, but realized she had lost so many points. She ran into the locker room and cried knowing that she wouldn't go on to the state championships. Nikki told her friend that she was going to quit gymnastics. Her friend gave her a card that said "you mustn't quit". She listened to her friend's advice and continued to train hard. The next year, Nikki did qualify for the state gymnastics championships.

This is just the beginning of Nikki's amazing story. After excelling in gymnastics, Nikki went on to become the America's first Olympic champion in inverted aerial skiing at the 1998 Winter Olympics in Nagano, Japan.

After a chronic back injury that left her unable to stand or walk, Nikki fought back by remembering her gymnastics experience. Her perseverance earned her 35 World Cup podiums, eleven World Cup titles, four national titles and two Overall World Grand Prix titles in addition to the Olympic gold medal. Nikki also applied her drive to succeed to college, earning a Magna Cum Laude degree from Union College in New York, and a Summa Cum Laude Master's Degree in Sports Psychology from the University of Utah, where she also taught as a visiting professor. Nikki earned these honors based on her college work (straight A's). Today, Nikki travels worldwide as an inspirational speaker, ski host, and sports psychology consultant.

Nikki's advice about perseverance for kids is:

"The biggest obstacle I overcame was my spinal injury. It is incredibly defeating when you can't sit for more than 30 minutes, can't stand for more than 15, and you have 10 doctors telling you to quit your sport and try to figure out something else to do with your life. I thought my lifelong dream could be over when I injured my spine. Then, I decided to prove all the doctors wrong, pushed through the pain to build the muscles in my back to support the injured disks, and returned to jumping 12 months later."

Daniel Fells (NFL)

Daniel Fells was born in 1983 in Anaheim, California, and attended nearby Fullerton High School. He was an All-Freeway League athlete in football, basketball and baseball, and received All-CIF honors in football and was his team's MVP. He also received All SoCal Hoops Division II-A honorable mention in basketball.

Daniel started his college football career at UC Davis as a wide receiver, but soon switched to play tight end, his NFL position. At the end of his freshman year of college, Daniel was told he couldn't play because he struggled with his grades. After taking courses at a community college, Daniel returned with his grades up and completed a successful college career. During his junior year at UC Davis, Daniel made the Great Western Football Conference all-conference team, with 35 receptions for 520 yards and 1 touchdown. Daniel then decided to follow his dream of playing in the NFL. He tried out for the Atlanta Falcons as an undrafted free agent in 2006: he made the roster. In 2009 and 2010 he had two successful seasons with the St. Louis Rams. In 2012, he signed with the New England Patriots as a tight end. Daniel's own sports hero is Magic Johnson.

Daniel told me:

"When I was in college at UC Davis, I was kicked out of school my second year due to bad grades. No school meant no football, and no future for me. It would have been easy for me to just accept that, move back home and look for a minimum wage job. But I wanted more. I had to pay my way through a community college for a semester, take online courses, and repeat a class I had failed in summer school. During spring break, I took a lifeguarding course, even though I am not a very good swimmer, because I could use those credits towards my re-enrollment. After busting my hump, I was reinstated at college, and got to play ball that year, and the rest is history."

Nicole Barnhart (Pro Soccer Player)

Nicole is one of America's top female soccer players. She played on the 2007 Women's World Cup and 2008 Olympic teams, and she is a volunteer coach for the Stanford women's soccer team.

Nicole's advice for kids about perseverance is:

"I played on boy's teams growing up, which was a challenge itself, but one that I think helped build me into the person and player I am today. When I first tried out for the State ODP (Olympic Development Program) team, I actually only made the B team, where I saw limited playing time. In high school, I was on the boy's team (we didn't have a girls team), and again, I didn't see much playing time. My freshman year of college, I think I played in a total of four games all season, and that was just a few odd minutes here and there. My sophomore year of college, I tore my ACL, so I missed that whole season. In 2006, I did not play in a single game for the national team. To start 2007, the year of the World Cup, I was not on contract or even in training camp with the national team. In May, 2008 (a month before they were naming the Olympic roster) I had knee surgery. Despite all of this, I made the World Cup Team, where we won bronze and I made the Olympic Team, where we won gold. Had I given up at any point in this journey where things were not going my way, I definitely would not be where I am today.

I know that many people will get angry, upset, frustrated, and down when things don't go well, they lose a game, or maybe they are not getting the playing time they think they deserve, but my message to them is that I have three times been a member of teams for world championship competitions. Despite not playing a single second, I helped our team in those events, and I have a silver and bronze medal from the World Cup, and a gold medal from the Olympics to show for it. And you know what else I have? Many amazing memories and friendships from the journey."

Consuella "Connie" Moore (Track & Field)

Growing up, Consuella "Connie" Moore was the fastest kid on her block. When she was about 10, she realized that no one in her neighborhood could catch her. She knew she was fast, but she said, "I really did not think much of it, I was just having fun."

Connie attended an inner-city high school in Chicago with 98 percent of students coming from low-income homes. During her time there, only a small percentage of students met the standards for reading and math in Illinois. Connie used her participation in track and field to keep focused. The faster she finished her school homework, the sooner she could get back on the track. Connie not only got straight A's, she graduated first in her high school class.

Penn State University was different. Connie referred to herself as a "book-worm" in high school, but she struggled in her first semester at college. She was declared ineligible to participate in track and field at Penn State because her grades had fallen.

She made a turnaround when she saw her fellow teammates suiting up and competing.

"I didn't know what it meant until that point when I saw my other team-mates competing without me," she explained. "Then I knew I had to do it, and I made that turnaround." The first time Connie stepped on the track in the blue and white Penn State uniform, she knew she had persevered. She compared her hard work on the field to the classroom.

"Athletes never back down from a challenge," Connie said. "It's the same thing in the classroom. If I could go through track practice every day and go through the tortures I go through in workouts, I could sit down and open up a book. It just reinforced my desire."

Later on, in college at Penn State University, Connie worked with kids with special needs through the Life Link program. She was a mentor to the kids, bringing them to the college campus, to sports events, and helping them with their education and life plans. Connie achieved a degree in psychology and then got an MBA in marketing.

Connie Moore gave me her advice about perseverance:

"Perseverance has been the story of my life. Every day my goal is to be better than I was the day before. Whether it is to be a better person, a better athlete, or a better friend, it is a daily perseverance. I grew up in inner city Chicago where drugs and violence ran rampant. Simply getting out of the neighborhood was a form of perseverance. When I was at Penn State University, I failed to meet the academic standards at the school. I was very tempted to drop out, go back to Chicago, and let my track and field career fall by the wayside. But instead I decided to work harder in my classes, train harder on the track and try to leave my mark in the Penn State history books. What happened is that I became an 11-time All American, 8-time Big Ten Champion and the first Penn State Olympian in women's track and field history. Because I worked harder in my classes, my schooling didn't stop there. I went on to get my MBA in Marketing."

Amy Hayes (Boxing - Ring Announcer)

How she persevered: Tried for almost ten years to become the first female boxing announcer and she succeeded!

Amy was born November 24, 1973 at Wyandotte General Hospital near Detroit, Michigan. She was a premature baby and battled croup and jaundice (two problems that can affect premature babies). She says she was as stubborn as a baby as she is today. Amy fought back to get healthy, even though she was so small at 5 pounds that her dad put her in a shoebox.

Amy loves her parents and says they are the biggest influences on her. Her dad taught her to be strong and get back up if she got knocked down.

Her dad taught her that "your word is all you have, and integrity and character are everything."

- It took her nearly 10 years to really get started as a boxing announcer.
- She is the first legitimate female announcer in boxing which was an "all boys club" before Amy started.
- She was ready to quit trying when she got a call from a promoter and got a five-year contract to be an announcer.
- She is the first female to announce a World Title Fight and work on television regularly as a boxing announcer.

Amy's advice for kids about perseverance:

"I was 18 years old when I wanted to become boxing's first female announcer. It took me 8 years or more to break through. By determination and tenacity, I finally bumped into a few good men who helped me become the first, most significant female announcer in the history of Boxing. I even got my own series, "Sunday Night Fights" on Fox Sports Net. Do not be afraid to take the road less traveled. Also, that's the title of a book worth reading, too!"

Jennifer Wester (Olympic and Pro Ice Dancer)

Jennifer Wester

Jennifer Wester is an Olympic and national champion ice dancer who has appeared on "Skating With the Stars" as the partner of Mötley Crüe singer Vince Neil. Before Jennifer became an ice skater, she was an eight-time national champion in a very different sport from ice dancing: silhouette sports shooting.

At age 11, she started ice skating to cross-train for her shooting competitions and she soon discovered she loved the ice. Jennifer is married to her ice dancing partner Daniil Barantsev. The pair have won numerous regional, national and international skating medals. Jennifer is also a graduate of Strayer University with a degree in marketing and speaks Italian, German and Russian.

When Jennifer told me this story, it reminded me of a lot of kids. Kids get teased in school every day.

"Other girls taunted me from the stands at a show early in my skating career. I still remember them laughing. I let them distract me, and consequently I fell in the middle of the rink in the middle of my performance.

Those same girls told me often that I was wasting my time and I would never get anywhere. But they were so distracted trying to rattle me, that it was their careers and talent that suffered. I stood up and continued my performance then, and every performance thereafter, in spite of those who told me I couldn't. It's about improving your own game, not about beating someone else. There will always be someone else that can be better, stronger, faster, or smarter. The question is, 'Will they be at their best when you are at yours?' And the only way you can navigate that question, is to always be at your best."

CHAPTER 2

Hard Work & Positive Attitude

Work (noun): sustained physical or mental effort to overcome obstacles and achieve an objective or result.

Attitude (noun): a feeling or emotion toward a fact or state.

The dictionary is the only place that success comes before work. Hard work is the price we must pay for success. I think you can accomplish anything if you're willing to pay the price.
-Green Bay Packers Coach Vince Lombardi

I know you've heard it a thousand times before. But it's true - hard work pays off. If you want to be good, you have to practice, practice, practice. If you don't love something, then don't do it.
-Author Ray Bradbury

Things turn out best for the people who make the best of the way things turn out. -UCLA Coach John Wooden

The greatest discovery of all time is that a person can change his future by merely changing his attitude.
-Oprah Winfrey

I completed over 500 interviews for TeensOnSports.com in about 18 months. It didn't feel like hard work. I was having too much of a good time. When I look back on how many interviews I did and how much I learned, I can see that it was a lot of hard work. I couldn't have done all the work if I had let myself get discouraged.

I made dozens of calls and sent dozens of e-mails before I heard back from a pro athlete, Brett Hull. Another way I learned about hard work and having a positive attitude was from the athletes themselves. No matter which sport they played or which position, every single athlete told me they had to work hard to achieve their goals. Every single athlete talked about the attitude they needed to achieve success. This chapter could be the longest in the book, because there isn't a top athlete in the world who hasn't worked hard, and whose attitude didn't make the difference between success and failure in their sports careers. I'm going to pick the best stories for you about hard work and positive attitude.

Kyle Busch (NASCAR)

Highlights: In 2010, Kyle became the first driver in NASCAR history to sweep the top three series: Sprint Cup, Nationwide, and Camping World Truck Series. Kyle had a record-setting 13 wins in the 2010 NASCAR Nationwide Series, has racked up 24 NASCAR Sprint Cup victories, and has a total of 104 wins in the three NASCAR series. His win record places him #3 on the all-time NASCAR winners list, behind only classic drivers Richard Petty (200) and David Pearson (106) wins.

Kyle Busch has been called "King of the Concrete," and in less than ten years, he has racked up many "firsts" in his career as a NASCAR driver. He was only 16 when he started competing in the Camping World Truck series in 2001. Kyle's young age even caused a slight controversy as NASCAR changed the minimum age limit for competition to 18, side-lining Kyle until he became old enough to compete again in the series. In 2004, Kyle became the youngest top rookie driver in NASCAR history.

Known as one of NASCAR's most dynamic drivers, Kyle won the Nation-wide Series Championship with the most points ever earned (5,682), most laps led (2,698), and most runner-up finishes (11) in one season.

Kyle's philosophy is "Win or go home." He brings the same strong philos-ophy to his new role as team owner of Kyle Busch Motorsports. Growing up, Kyle's heroes were his dad and brother, who were also racers. Kyle's brother Kurt was the 2004 Nextel Cup Series champion and his father was NASCAR driver Tom Busch. Kyle's favorite NASCAR drivers when he was growing up were Jeff Gordon and Dale Earnhardt. He even dressed like Jeff Gordon for Halloween.

Kyle would never be where he is today without hard work. He told me that hard work "means everything. You can't just expect to go out there and win on talent alone. People have the misconception that my brother and I were given everything, but that couldn't be more the opposite. When we raced, if we wrecked a car, we were going to pay for it and put it back together ourselves before we got to race again. I think a great example of hard work would be my crew chief Dave Rogers. There isn't anyone in the garage that's going to outwork the guy. I follow his example, and hopefully that turns into a Sprint cup championship someday for the both of us."

Ryan Palmer (PGA Golfer)

Ryan Palmer (credit – Orasi Sports)

Highlights: 3 PGA wins, 5 second place finishes, and has finished in the top ten 22 times, earning over $11 million on the tour. He qualified for the prestigious 2010 Masters in Augusta, Georgia by winning the Sony Open in Hawaii.

Growing up, Ryan Palmer loved baseball, basketball and golf. Ryan says that he didn't choose golf, "it chose him." He didn't improve much in baseball and quit playing basketball after his sophomore year in high school. He never quit playing golf.

Ryan won his first golf tournament when he was 10 years old near his hometown of Amarillo, TX. In high school, he played all day long with his teammates Ty Cox and Matt Watson. They played up to 45 holes in a day. That's a lot of golf! In addition to a 10+ year career on the PGA golf tour, Ryan Palmer and his wife Jennifer started the Ryan Palmer Foundation. Ryan's foundation supports young golfers who need help with green fees and equipment and has paid hundreds of thousands of dollars for children's hospitals and medical care.

Ryan talked to me about having a positive attitude and working hard. His great attitude and hard work have paid off. He jumped over 150 places in the golf rankings by winning the Sony Open in Hawaii in 2010.

Ryan said, "Let's just say that if I'm not positive and excited when I'm on the course, I may as well be at home doing something else. In the game of golf, you have to believe in yourself and your ability to pull off each and every shot. There will come a time during a round when you struggle, but the player who can stay positive and believe in himself will overcome whatever is thrown at him during a round of golf.

A positive attitude is crucial in whatever line of work you are in. I don't care how hard you work or think you work, there is always someone working just as hard, if not harder. It takes a lot of time and discipline in whatever sport or business you pursue. I have won 3 times on the PGA tour, but there is a lot I could improve on. I'm working every day trying to get better. Whether its spending time in the gym, or on the range, I'm always working to get better. It just takes hard work to improve in everything you do."

Kevin "Special K" Daley (Harlem Globetrotters Basketball)

Like millions of others, Kevin Daley's hero has always been Michael Jordan. Kevin didn't just get to meet Michael Jordan, he got to be Michael Jordan. He starred in a sports drink commercial that featured Michael Jordan playing one-on-one against his younger self. Only the younger self wasn't Michael Jordan, it was Kevin Daley.

Kevin dropped out of college to join the Harlem Globetrotters, the world's most famous basketball team, but when he did it, he made a promise to himself that he'd finish his college degree.

Kevin talked to me about what having a positive attitude has done for him:

"I believe that my attitude transfers to the crowd, so that's why I am always upbeat. I always have fun because I want them to forget about any bad things that are happening in their life. If I have a bad attitude, something bad could happen. When something is going bad, I find something good to pull out of it.

There are not many people in life that are successful without hard work. Some people do get lucky or know somebody in the right place. The majority of people need to work hard to be successful. There are many people who wish they had my position right now, and there are people who are trying to take my position right now, and therefore, I need to always work hard. Without the hard work I would not be here today."

In addition to playing hundreds of games, Kevin kept the promise he made to himself when he started playing for the Globetrotters. He received his bachelor's degree from Ashford University in 2011 with a 3.6 GPA at the same time as he played more than 500 games in 25 countries, 150 US cities, traveling over 50,000 miles.

Jim Kyte (Retired NHL Player)

"Legend of Hockey" Jim Kyte was one of the biggest, strongest defense players in the National Hockey League. In his long career, Jim played nearly 600 games for five teams, and was renowned for his talent and commitment to the game. Jim is also the only legally deaf person to every play in the National Hockey League, much less as a top pro for fifteen years.

Jim's hard work and positive attitude are linked together.

He told me, "As a legally deaf person, I had many people tell me I couldn't accomplish something because of my deafness. I always silently told myself, 'just watch me.' This confidence was rooted in the fact that I grew up in a family of five boys plus my father all wearing hearing aids, so there wasn't much sympathy. My father said we may have a handicap but it is not a disability. We can accomplish anything we set our minds to. One specific time I can share with you is something all athletes face – a case of shaken self-confidence. I was fortunate to be a 1st round draft choice for the Winnipeg Jets in 1982, but early in my career, I was not getting a lot of ice time. The coach had a difficult time having confidence in me because I was making too many rookie mistakes. I became so terrified of making a mistake that I didn't want to handle the puck and my overall confidence started to dwindle. I finally realized that if I played 'afraid' (of making a mistake) I was definitely going to find myself on the end of the bench. However, if I played the way I knew I could and happened to make a mistake along the way, I might, or might not, end up on the end of the bench. This was a small but very important distinction to me. I started to play 'unafraid,' regained my confidence, and in turn, the coach started showing confidence in me by giving me more ice time and opportunities to play in key situations. The rest is history."

About having a positive attitude, Jim said,

"A positive attitude is more important than skill, knowledge or ability, particularly in team sports. Nobody wants to listen to negativity. As the saying goes, whether you think you can or you can't, you're right. Always be positive no matter what situation you or your team faces. There is no substitute for hard work on or off the playing surface. High performers reap rewards over non-performers because of their strong work ethic. I truly believe you play the way you practice – you just can't turn up the effort level for game situations and expect to be a high performer. Someone who studies for a math test by doing their homework regularly will always out-perform someone who just crams the night before. I'm a firm believer in the 5 P's – Proper Preparation Prevents Poor Performance."

Brittney Palmer (MMA Ring Girl and Artist)

Brittney Palmer (credit – Compliments of Brittney Palmer)

Brittney Palmer is one of the most popular MMA ring girls, and is also an artist and multi-talented entertainer. In 2009, Brittney took a break from being a ring girl to return to school and develop her art talent. She returned to MMA after popular demand in December, 2011. Brittney also volunteers for the USO/Armed Forces Entertainment program, which brings entertainment to U.S. troops serving around the world.

Brittney told me, "I'm in an industry where you're rejected as much you're accepted. It doesn't matter if you win the title shot in MMA, you're still going to take your lumps along the way. Being positive is as important as anything you do physically. This is true for other things, too. As soon as you doubt that you can paint a challenging painting, you won't be able to. The way you approach a task is directly related to your success! It's a cliché, but hard work pays off. Another cliché that's very true is that nothing comes easy. If it's worth your time and energy, you have to approach it that way and do everything to attain it. Hard work is the foundation of success."

Randy Wells (MLB)

Randy Wells is a pitcher for the Chicago Cubs. He became the first Cubs pitcher since Kerry Woods to win at least seven games in a rookie season. I had the opportunity to meet and interview him during a youth baseball clinic in St. Louis. He taught the participants specific skills in baseball, but more importantly he taught them life lessons. The conversation focused mostly on the impact of hard work on success in sports and life.

Randy told me, "If you want to take it to the next level, it all depends on you. How much you want it and how much work you are willing to put in. Give it everything you've got and don't ever take 'no' for an answer. If someone says you can't do it, work harder and prove them wrong."

Jennifer Barretta (Billiards/Professional Pool Player)

Jennifer Barretta is a very successful Billiard player. Her nickname is "9mm Barretta". She lives in New York with her husband and child. Jennifer turned pro in 2003 and has been competing ever since. She was featured in a pool documentary in 2009.

She shared her thoughts about the importance of working hard, "If you're trying to be a pro athlete, you have to remember that when you are laying around playing video games or watching TV, someone else is out there doing practice drills and getting better. You have to out work 99% of the competition to get to the top."

CHAPTER 3

Honesty & Integrity

Honesty (noun): fairness and straightforwardness of conduct.

Integrity (noun): adherence to moral principles, and an honest character.

Always tell the truth. That way, you don't have to remember what you said.
-Mark Twain

Honesty is the first chapter in the book of wisdom.
-Thomas Jefferson

Keep true, never be ashamed of doing right, decide on what you think is right and stick to it. -Author George Eliot

It's hard to be a sports fan and not hear stories about athletes taking performance-enhancing drugs and not admitting it. Some of the most popular athletes have been caught up in telling stories about taking these drugs. Other times, it's come out they have been dishonest with family or with friends.

But I've interviewed more than 500 athletes and none of them have been involved in a big scandal. What came across most to me in all of the interviews was how much they all emphasized telling the truth and treating their teammates, family and friends with respect. For every bad story we hear, there are dozens of top athletes who are honest, straightforward, and who treat others by the "Golden Rule" – which means you should treat others the way you would like them to treat you. The person who said this most clearly was Hall of Fame baseball pitcher Rich "Goose" Gossage

Rich "Goose" Gossage (MLB Hall of Fame)

Rich Gossage played 21 seasons of Major League Baseball for nine different teams, with his top years played for the New York Yankees, who won the World Series, and winning the National League championship with the San Diego Padres. Boasting one of the fastest pitches in baseball, "Goose" Gossage was a dominating relief pitcher, leading the AL in saves for several years. Gossage pitched in nine All-Star games and three World Series.

The "Goose" earned his nickname when he started in the major leagues for the Chicago White Sox in 1972. Goose's teammate Tom Bradley said he looked like a goose leaning over to get signs from the catcher and the nickname stuck. He returned to his hometown of Colorado Springs, CO after retiring as a pitcher and continues to be active promoting youth sports. The Rich "Goose" Gossage Youth Sports complex in Colorado Springs has five youth baseball and softball fields dedicated to the fiery fastball pitcher who pitched over 1,000 games, finishing 681 games, and earning 310 saves.

This legend of baseball and Hall of Famer had a reputation as a "wild man" when he played baseball. But he emphasized that you didn't get anywhere by treating people poorly.

He said, "Integrity develops by how you treat people and conduct yourself with teammates. You treat the people the way you want to be treated. You don't go out on the field or anywhere else treating people like a jerk."

George Wilson (NFL)

George Wilson (credit – Buffalo Bills)

George Wilson got started in football in the fourth grade. He lived with his mom Wanda and older brother Kiyo in the small town of Paducah, KY. His older brother played football and George loved the game. George decided that he didn't just want to play football in school, he wanted to play in the NFL. He asked God every night, "Help me to take a step toward seeing my dream come true." He made a deal with God. "If you bless me to see my dream come true, I won't be selfish. I'll share my testimony with anybody willing to listen."

As safety for the Buffalo Bills since 2005, George got the attention of football fans in his first starting game in 2007, when he intercepted a pass from Tony Romo on Monday Night Football and carried the ball all the way to the goal line for a touchdown.

A star on and off the football field, George kept his promise to God and shares his message with young people as a sought-after motivational speaker for his own George Wilson S.A.F.E.T.Y. Foundation. George was also named the Walter Payton Man of the Year for the Bills in 2009.

George Wilson has been voted team captain for the Buffalo Bills two years in a row. He talked to me about leadership and integrity:

"A leader has to lead by example first and foremost, so that when he does speak he's already done the work and shown his guys how to do it. That way when he does speak his words have merit. If somebody just does a lot of talking without actions behind the words, they are only hollow words and guys are only going to follow that leader for so long. A leader has to lead by example. You have to have integrity. The guys have to trust you. You have to be accountable. You have to be responsible. I know those are a lot of attributes of a leader but all of those things are imperative if you want to be an effective leader."

David Gilliland (NASCAR)

David Gilliland (credit – Breaking Limits LLC)

A lot of people don't associate Southern California with stock car racing, but David Gilliland grew up in the Riverside, CA race shop of his father, NASCAR Winston West driver Butch Gilliland. NASCAR is a sport for drivers and mechanics, and David learned how to work on cars during his high school years, and was his dad's crew chief when he was only 19 years old. In 1997 when David was only 21, his dad won the Winston West series and David became the Champion Crew Chief of the year.

The next year, David started racing at the Perris, CA dirt track, winning two races. By the next year, he won 9 of the 15 races at the Perris track. He put his own team together and raced on the Irwindale, CA speedway the next year, and advanced to the NASCAR Grand National West Series. In 2006, he advanced to national-level NASCAR competition in the Nation-wide and Sprint Cup series. That year, David scored an unprecedented upset win at the Kentucky Speedway, entering the June 18, 2006 Nation-wide NASCAR race as a total unknown driving for a part-time team owned by Clay Andrews. Five seconds behind leader J.J. Yeley with only 10 laps left, David passed Yeley to take the lead and the checkered flag. He went from unknown West Coast driver to being one of the most sought-after young NASCAR professionals.

In 2007, David's biggest success to date came with starting at the pole position at one of the biggest races ever, the Daytona 500. In 2009, David raced for TRG Motorsports, and then moved to Front Row Motorsports in 2010.

David told me that in 2009, two weeks before Daytona (the start of the season) he found out he didn't have a ride. He had to watch the Daytona 500 race on TV instead of competing.

David said, "It was a tough situation and it was a tough season that year. I think I drove for eight or nine different people throughout the year. There were times when I'd go home and wonder, 'Man, do I need to be doing something else?'" He got through it, and he's glad that he did.

About honesty, David said, "I think honesty and integrity play a big role in everyday life – in sports or anything you do. If you have those traits, it makes you a better person and it helps you do whatever you're doing better."

Shahar Pe'er (Pro Tennis Player)

Shahar Pe'er is the top-ranked Israeli singles tennis player of all time among both men and women. She reached number 11 among tennis players worldwide in 2011.

Shahar's mother Aliza and father Dovik were both athletic. Her father was the swimming champion of the city of Jerusalem and her mother a champion runner. Shahar started playing tennis along with her brother and sister when she was only six years old. Her brother and sister stopped playing tennis as teens, but Shahar kept playing.

By age 10, Shahar was following a tough schedule of practice, school, more practice after school, then homework. She got up at 5:30 every morning and didn't stop tennis practice until 8:00 every night. At age 12, she won the international junior women's double title along with Nicole Vaidisova, reaching the world junior singles final playing on her own.

As a young Israeli, Shahar also experienced something that most kids around the world do not. All Israelis must serve in the military when they turn 18. Shahar served for two years in the Israeli military from 2005 to 2007. She was able to participate in a program that allows athletes to continue to compete at the same time as they do their military service. Shahar also experienced controversy while playing on the international pro tennis circuit. In 2009, because she is an Israeli, she was not allowed to play in a tennis tournament in Dubai. Top players including Venus Williams and Andy Roddick withdrew from the tournament to protest. The next year, Shahar was allowed to compete in Dubai, but with severe restrictions. She had to exercise in a separate gym and was under guard at all times. Venus Williams said, "I can't imagine playing so well under the circumstances. She's courageous. I don't think anyone else on the tour could do what she's doing." Shahar has won 5 women's tennis titles and been runner-up in three other WTA tournaments.

Shahar has earned the respect of her competitors on the pro tennis tour. She told me, "I think that for anyone to be a good athlete you should first of all be a good person. And for me it is very important to have integrity. I try always to respect my fans, my opponents and my coaches and family."

Devon Harris (Olympic Bobsledder)

Everyone may not know the name of Devon Harris, but they know the pusher and team captain of the famous Jamaican Bobsled team that competed in the Olympics in 1988, 1992 and 1998. The story of the team's impossible dream that came true is the basis for the Disney film "Cool Runnings."

Today, Devon Harris is a successful motivational speaker who tells people to "keep on pushing" just as he did on the Jamaican bobsled team. Devon grew up in a poor, violent neighborhood in Kingston, the capital of Jamaica. Devon was able to attend the Royal Military Academy, Sandhurst, in England and served as an officer in the Jamaican Defence Force. It was while serving as an officer in the Jamaican military that the idea of a Jamaican bobsled team originated. He tried out for the team and was chosen to compete in their first winter Olympic Games in Calgary, Canada.

Growing up, Devon looked around at his violent neighborhood and decided that a positive attitude and a "never say die" philosophy would carry him farther than taking on a sense of injustice and filling his heart with anger. Today, his message is that perseverance can help all people to overcome obstacles and achieve their dreams. He is the founder of the Keep on Pushing Foundation which promotes education for kids in disadvantaged communities. Devon is also involved with the international Right to Play movement, which encourages play and physical activity for children around the world. He is also an author of a children's book and his motivational book, Keep on Pushing: Hot Lessons from Cool Runnings.

Devon is one of the most positive, highly-motivational people in the world. He talked to me about honesty and integrity, and how important they are in sports and in life.

"I regard sports as perhaps the 'fairest' kind of competitive activity we can participate in. You are pitting your natural athletic talents, determination, drive and courage against the next person's and the results of that head to head is reflected on the scoreboard. Honesty and integrity are keys to keep that purity in sports. Cheating of any kind really violates the idea of fairness and level playing field."

Haloti Ngata (NFL)

Haloti Ngata (credit – Phil Hoffmann, Ravens)

Giant, dominant defensive end for the Baltimore Ravens, Haloti Ngata (pronounced "Nahta"), has emerged as a centerpiece of the Ravens defense. Recognized as one of the best defensive tackles in the league, Haloti is modest about his success. Even though coaches and sports journalists refer to him as gifted, outstanding, and intelligent, Haloti gives his fellow players credit for his achievements. He says he learned how to play the run from Kelly Gregg and learned his pass-rush moves from Trevor Pryce (formerly of the Ravens defensive line, now with the New York Jets). Haloti has even been called "The NFL's Incredible Hulk."

Haloti has overcome personal hardship in his rise to the top of his football game. When he started playing college football for Oregon in 2002, his father Solomone, a truck driver, was leaving from a visit with Haloti. He lost control of his truck and was killed when the truck overturned and went into a canal. Haloti's mother Olga grew so depressed after Solomone's death that her health suffered and Haloti left school to care for her. Haloti's mother Olga entered the hospital on January 1, 2006, but suffered a heart attack while undergoing treatment and died.

Haloti's high school football coach said that he grew up during these difficult times. His main priority became taking care of his family. Now, Haloti and his wife Christina have a young son, Sam. Haloti is of Tongan ancestry and his cousins Fili and Sifa Moala are also talented athletes. Fili is a defensive lineman for the Indianapolis Colts, and Sifa is a starting guard for the University of Nevada - Las Vegas.

Everything that Haloti told me matches his personal story. When we talked about honesty and integrity, he said,

"When my dad passed away, I felt like I lost my biggest fan. I had to learn to really lean on God and lean on family and friends. They helped me get through it. Integrity is huge in everything that we do. If you're not ever going to cover your teammate's back, there's never going to be a team. All those things play a big role in being a great team."

CHAPTER 4

Leadership & Teamwork

Leadership (noun): The capacity to lead.

Example is not the main thing in influencing others, it is the only thing.
-Albert Schweitzer

Leadership and learning are indispensable to each other.
-John F. Kennedy

I think that being a leader means being an example for others, first of all. Not everyone wants to step up and act like a leader. Sometimes it just happens. You start doing something, and you realize that everyone else is following your example. When you're on the field playing sports, the team naturally looks toward one or two players as the leaders. Leadership is a part of human nature. Sometimes we need to step up and take the lead, and other times, we look to others for our examples and we follow their leadership.

Athletes are accustomed to being leaders in their sport. Sometimes they are looked to as leaders and role models in the rest of life, too. At the same time, it seems like hardly a day goes by when we don't hear disappointing examples of athletes who were leaders and role models who didn't live up to the image that people had of them. One thing I learned while interviewing all the athletes was that for every star athlete who has a negative story, there are so many athletes who not only live up to the image that people have of them, they live above and beyond that image. These athletes are humble, kind, true team players, and every day leaders.

Mark Munoz (MMA Fighter)

Mark Munoz (credit – Tracy Lee)

Mark Munoz AKA "The Filipino Wrecking Machine," was born on a U.S. military base in Yokosuka, Japan, and moved with his parents to Vallejo, California when he was 2 years old. He won the California State High School Wrestling championship two times, and was the 1998 NHSCA National High School champion. He went to Oklahoma State University, where he continued to excel as a wrestler, winning two Big 12 wrestling titles and two All-America honors, as well as the NCAA wrestling title as a college senior. Mark graduated from Oklahoma State with a Bachelors degree in Health Science.

Mark entered Mixed Martial Arts fighting in 2007. He is one of the fastest-rising MMA stars, currently ranked #4 middleweight in the world. Mark would be a wrestling coach for kids if he was not fighting in the UFC. He continues to coach high school athletes in a 5 to 10 day wrestling camp in Oceanside, California every year.

What Mark told me about leadership seems very true to me. Mark said that the best leaders had humility, initiative, perseverance, and assertiveness. Leaders should have enough humility to know that they can always improve upon every performance. Mark said that we must be able to learn even though we are very good at something. Other qualities of great leaders that Mark mentioned were the initiative to take action immediately when you see something that needs to be corrected. "Being assertive as a leader is a must," Mark said. "Leaders must take action and voice their opinion even when others don't want to hear."

Keith Tkachuk (Retired NHL Player)

While playing for the St. Louis Blues from 2001-2010, Keith Tkachuk was nicknamed "Big Walt," because he was so dominating in front of the net, and so imposing as a player. Keith began playing hockey in high school, and was a member of the U.S. National Junior Hockey Team and the 1992 U.S. Olympic Hockey Team.

Immediately after he played in the Olympics, Keith started playing pro hockey for the Winnipeg Jets. He spent most of his professional hockey career as an outstanding player for the St. Louis Blues, where he achieved the coveted milestone of 1,000 points in 2008. Keith also played in five NHL All-Star games.

Keith responded to his interview very similarly to the way he played the game: straightforward, and straight-ahead. When I asked him who he felt was a great leader, he immediately brought up Chris Chelios, former NHL player who had the longest active playing career of any NHL player. Chris played from 1983 to 2010. Chris was Captain of the Chicago Blackhawks from 1995 to 1999, and led Team USA to its 1996 World Cup of Hockey victory over Canada.

As a big, strong player, Keith singled out Chris Chelios' leadership capabilities, "Because he wasn't the biggest but he competed and made everyone else he played with play harder." Coming from a man who outweighed Chelios by over 40 pounds and who was an opposing player, the praise really meant a lot.

Sarah Kaufman (MMA Fighter)

Sarah Kaufman is the first and only Hardcore Championship Fighting Women's Bantamweight Champion. She also won the Strikeforce Women's Bantamweight Championship in 2010. Sarah has a brown belt in Brazilian Jiu-Jitsu, but she was originally a dancer who performed all types of dance, from jazz to ballet to hip-hop. She attended two years at the University of Victoria, BC, with a goal of being a cardiovascular surgeon. Sarah won her first 10 fights, seven by knockout. Sarah is consistently in the top 10 rankings of female MMA fighters in the world.

When Sarah was 17, she started taking MMA classes with Adam Zugec when he opened his MMA training studio in her hometown of Victoria, B.C. Now, she teaches classes at the Zugec martial arts studio. Sarah told me, "In order to be a leader you need to be respected for your integrity, work ethic and knowledge. I believe you also need to be working with a group of people you trust wholeheartedly and who feel the same about you. Being a leader is about being able to work well in a group, but for me it's developing a familial connection that enables me to lead to the best of my ability."

Chase Coffman (NFL)

Chase Coffman's career as an NFL tight end is just beginning, but he excelled in football in high school and college. Chase comes from a famous football family. His father Paul Coffman was a tight end for the Green Bay Packers and Kansas City Chiefs between 1978 and 1987. Chase's younger brother Carson is the starting quarterback for the Kansas State University Wildcats. Chase set numerous records as a tight end at Raymore-Peculiar High School, earning first team All-State honors, and winning the Simone Award of the year for catching 41 passes and scoring 16 touchdowns. He was a college all-American for the University of Missouri Tigers and led the team with numerous records as a tight end.

Chase emphasized trust, preparation and inspiration for good leaders when I talked to him. He said, "Good leaders get people to believe in them. People believe good leaders will always try their best, by hard work and preparation or inspiration, to put their followers in the best position to succeed."

Megan LaTempt (NFL Cheerleader)

Megan LaTempt

Megan LaTempt was a cheerleader and dance team member throughout high school and college in Missouri. She decided she wanted to be a cheerleader for the St. Louis Rams since she performed a dance routine at the Pro Bowl while she was a 14 year-old middle school student. Megan graduated from Southeast Missouri State University with a degree in exceptional child education, and began teaching special education students at St. Genevieve, Missouri. She was teaching full time when she tried out for the St. Louis Rams cheerleading squad in 2009, and made it. Within a year, Megan became a captain of the St. Louis Rams cheerleading squad. She continues to teach special education students and now supervises seven other teachers.

Megan has been a leader as a teacher and a cheerleader. She told me that "Teamwork, loyalty, and cooperation are very important in a cheer/dance team because if you do not have these character items, you would not have a team for long. Each item goes hand in hand with the next and all must be present in order to have success in your organization."

CHAPTER 5

Character Role Model

Character (noun): one of the attributes or features that make up and distinguish an individual.

Role model (noun): a person whose behavior in a particular role is imitated by others.

Celebrity-worship and hero-worship should not be confused. Yet we confuse them every day, and by doing so we come dangerously close to depriving ourselves of real role models. We lose sight of the men and women who do not simply seem great because they are famous but are famous because they are great. We come closer and closer to degrading all fame into notoriety.
-Historian and Librarian of Congress Daniel J. Boorstin

Be more concerned with your character than your reputation, because your character is what you really are, while your reputation is merely what others think you are. -UCLA Coach John Wooden

When I started interviewing athletes, it was a little bit intimidating. I wasn't sure how they would react, and nearly everyone I talked to was a sports hero to me. One of the questions I asked the athletes was "Who is the best character person in your life?" I wanted to find out who inspired them. I found out that most athletes looked very close to home.

Just like everyone else, their role models were their moms, their dads, and sometimes even their kids. Athletes are great role models when they stay true to themselves. As UCLA Coach John Wooden said, "Your character is who you really are." I think so many of the athletes said that their family or friends were their best character role models because they knew their friends and family the best. When we are lucky enough to have great people in our families and have great friends, this is all the foundation that we need for success.

Kevin Durant (NBA)

Kevin Durant (credit – Noah Graham/NBAE/Getty Images)

Kevin Durant was born in Washington, D.C. in 1988. He plays for the Oklahoma City Thunder in the NBA. Kevin has been an extremely successful basketball player in all levels of play. In high school, he was named first team All-American by USA Today and PARADE Magazine. While attending the University of Texas, he was recognized by several organizations as the national player of the year. Kevin was also named the MVP of the Big 12 Tournament.

Kevin was drafted 2nd overall in the 2007 NBA entry draft by the Seattle Supersonics. The Seattle Supersonics moved to Oklahoma City in 2008 and became the Thunder. In 2008, Kevin won the NBA rookie of the year award. He has been named to the NBA all-star team three times. In the 2009-10 season, he became the youngest player in NBA history to win the scoring title at age 22.

Kevin Durant is a very positive person and a great role model for kids. He is not one that will be caught up in controversy or getting into trouble. Kevin explained what he does outside of basketball, "I'm a homebody. I don't go out too much, so I enjoy hanging out with my friends and family. I enjoy music - I like to create my own sounds and beats. I also like interacting with all of my fans on Facebook and Twitter."

Kevin is a hero to others as well, based on his amazing abilities on the court, but more importantly, because of the many charities that he supports. He helps to raise money and awareness for - people in Haiti, holiday shopping for needy children, Parkinson's research, opportunities for Native American and Aboriginal youth to have access to physical activity and sports, and other important causes. Kevin also recently launched the Kevin Durant Family Foundation, which will host an annual KD35 Charity Ball.

When asked about his heroes growing up and those that impacted his character he responded by saying, "My mother was my hero growing up. She always worked real hard to make sure my older brother and I were taken care of."

Brett Hull (NHL Hall of Fame)

Brett Hull and his father Bobby Hull are the only father and son National Hockey League players to each score 1,000 points and to each be inducted into the Hockey Hall of Fame. Hull was the first athlete who called me back when I asked for an interview. He was #1 on the ice as a hockey player many times and he will always be #1 with "That's Great Advice."

Brett is one of hockey's all-time scoring leaders with 741 career goals. He has been called one of the "most feared" scorers in NHL history, because he could score at any time, and at his best, was impossible to defend against.

Brett Hull's nickname was "The Golden Brett," inspired by his father Bobby Hull's nickname, "The Golden Jet." Although his father was one of the most famous hockey players in the world, it was his mother Joanne, a professional figure skater, who taught Brett how to ice skate when he was five years old. He started playing hockey at age seven, and while in school, played hockey, baseball and football. Brett attended the University of Minnesota in Duluth, and in 1986, was a starring player on the Team USA Olympic hockey team. Brett started playing professional hockey for the Calgary Flames, but soon joined the St. Louis Blues, where he grew to be one of the NHL's best players, ultimately scoring an astounding 86 goals for the NHL's third-highest number of goals in one season.

Brett told me that one of his best friends was his best character role model. Kelly Chase was an NHL "enforcer" and also played as a right wing for the St. Louis Blues. According to Brett, Kelly was a great guy to play with as a teammate, a really good character guy, and a great family guy.

Brett told me that Kelly was having tough times struggling with a serious illness, but never worried about himself. Instead, Kelly had a great attitude and was always taking care of others. Brett said, "I aspire to be half the man that Kelly is." After his own NHL career, Kelly Chase went on to be a successful broadcaster for the St. Louis Blues. Both Kelly and Brett support many charitable activities benefiting children and sports.

Brittany Lincicome (LPGA Golfer)

Brittany Lincicome

Brittany Lincicome started playing golf when she was 9 years old, and won her first amateur golf tournament the same year. Her winning percentage as an amateur golfer is an amazing 60 percent. Her best LPGA score of 61 is a score that many male golfers would love to have. She is one of the longest, strongest drivers on the LPGA tour. Brittany took first place in LPGA driving distance at 296.0 yards. She has earned $4,432,000 so far playing professional golf.

Brittany told me that she had a hard time limiting her role models to just one. Finally, she said, "If I had to pick one, I'll pick a duo: my parents.

They taught me honesty and integrity, and also how to have fun in all I do. The biggest thing they did for me was to just love me."

Fred Lynn (Retired MLB Player)

In 1974, Fred Lynn was called up to the major leagues for the Boston Red Sox, and managed to have one of the best rookie seasons in MLB history. He ended the year by leading the Red Sox to the World Series, and received the MVP, Golden Glove and Rookie of the Year Awards.

Fred was born in Chicago, but his parents moved to Southern California when he was a year old. His baseball heroes were home run hitters Willie Mays and Roberto Clemente. He excelled in Little League, Pony League, and as a high school athlete. Fred set the goal of being the first person in his family to attend college, and although he was drafted by the New York Yankees straight out of high school, he went to USC on not a baseball, but a football scholarship. Although he played well on the USC Trojans football team, he switched to baseball during his sophomore year.

Fred Lynn is one of MLB's best-hitting centerfielders, only slightly behind legends like Willie Mays, Mickey Mantle, and Joe DiMaggio. Although he experienced injuries that meant that he was never quite able to equal his fantastic rookie season, Fred Lynn has more than 1,100 RBIs, 1,906 hits, and 306 career home runs.

Fred's parents were divorced when he was young, and he was raised by his father. When I asked him who his best role models were, he answered immediately: "My dad. He taught me how to play sports. We always played together. When I got to USC, my coach Rod Dado was my role model. He is the one who taught me the ins and outs of baseball and I followed his examples."

Dustin Brown (NHL)

Dustin Brown with Matthew

Dustin Brown became the youngest NHL team captain ever for the Los Angeles Kings in 2008. National Hockey League teams traditionally elect captains who are Canadian. Dustin became the first American-born player to be elected Kings team captain. Dustin was selected in the first draft round by the Kings in 2003. Dustin also played on the bronze medalist US Hockey team at the 2004 World Championships in Prague, Czech Republic.

Dustin is married to Nicole Brown. They have three sons, Jacob, Mason and Cooper, who are all under age five. Dustin is an explosive player whose play electrifies the ice. He signed one of hockey's most lucrative contracts with the L.A. Kings in 2007, a $19.5 million contract to play for the team until the 2014-2015 season.

When I asked Dustin who his best character role model was, he answered right away. "My wife," he said. "We have three small children and she is often left to deal with all the day to day stuff by herself. I know it isn't easy, but she makes it look easy. Our three boys are well mannered and great kids. A lot of that has to do with Nicole. No matter how hard it gets, she is always doing the best for my boys and our family."

Chipper Jones (MLB)

Chipper Jones

Chipper Jones is one of the best baseball players of this generation. He has been a pro for almost 20 years on the Atlanta Braves. Chipper has almost 500 home runs and a career batting average over .300. There are few professional athletes these days that play an entire career with one team. Chipper has announced his retirement to be effective at the end of the 2012 season. This will ensure that he only wore one uniform as a professional player.

I asked him about who his role models and heroes were growing up. His response was, "My parents are obviously the ones I looked up to for guidance, support and they helped mold me into the man and dad I am today. On the baseball side, I loved Cal (Ripken) and Ozzie (Smith). I emulated everything they did on the field as shortstops."

CHAPTER 6

Anti-Bullying & Dealing with a Bully

Bully (noun): A person who uses strength or power to harm or intimidate those who are weaker

Bullying (verb): Use superior strength or influence to intimidate (someone), typically to force him or her to do what one wants.

You, with your words like knives and swords and weapons that you use against me. -Taylor Swift (Lyric from *Mean*)

I enjoy most things about being in school - friends, volunteering, sports, teachers and coaches, and learning new information. At the same time, there is one major thing that I do not like - bullying. Some students pick on others, put others down, or do hurtful things. The purpose behind these behaviors appears to be to make the bully feel better about himself or herself at the expense of another.

When I started school I had some difficulty with speech. Some kids thought it was funny and made fun of the way I pronounced words. This made me feel bad and for a while I didn't want to speak up or share my ideas in class. Sometimes it felt as though the more upset I got, the worse the teasing became. My parents both gave me different advice. My dad is an elementary school principal and his advice was to ignore the behavior or to report this to a counselor, teacher, or the principal. My mom's advice was to stick up for myself and to show the bully that I wasn't going to tolerate this. I am really not sure that any one approach would have completely stopped the teasing, but I did try a little bit of each of these. Things did get better and eventually my speech improved. I also started training in Brazilian Jiu-Jitsu. I knew that fighting wouldn't solve the problem, but this did help build my confidence. I also knew that I would be prepared if someone did try to take me down.

This experience helped me to know what it feels like to be bullied and picked on. I decided that I would not want anyone else to feel the way that I did. I work very hard to stick up for those who are being bothered by others.

This past year I planned and led two anti-bullying assemblies in my school district for elementary students. My hope was that if we shared these messages with younger students, then we could help stop this problem before it starts. I am very grateful to MMA fighter Tyron Woodley and pro boxer Ryan Coyne who participated in these assemblies. It was interesting that two athletes who fight for a living had such great advice against bullying, strategies for dealing with bullies, and avoiding fights.

Tyron Woodley (MMA Fighter)

Tyron Woodley with Matthew

Tyron Woodley was born in a suburb of St. Louis, MO. He is the eleventh of thirteen children. Tyron's dad left at an early age so he was primarily raised by his mother. He was a successful football player and wrestler in high school. Tyron was on the honor roll every semester in high school. He was the Missouri state wrestling champion in high school. Tyron received many offers to wrestle in college but chose to go to the University of Missouri to help build-up the program. He was teammates with USA Olympian and Bellator MMA fighter Ben Askren. Together they helped Missouri develop a successful wrestling program.

After his career at Missouri, Tyron Woodley started his career in mixed martial arts. He has won his first 12 fights. Tyron has notable wins over Jordan Mein, Paul Daley, and Tarec Saffiedine. He appeared as a guest on the MTV2 Show *Bully Beatdown*. Tyron is the owner of ATT Evolution gym in suburban St. Louis.

Tyron came to my school to talk about positive character and anti-bullying. I asked him about his thoughts on bullies and bullying. His response was, "There were bullies when I was growing up. Bullies will find something to pick on people about. It could be the clothes you wear, the way you speak, or something about your appearance. You have to be confident in yourself. Nobody can make you feel any way that you don't want to feel. Don't hang around anyone who makes you feel bad. Make friends with people who are positive influences in your life."

Ryan Coyne (Pro Boxer)

Ryan Coyne grew up in St. Charles, Missouri. He was a top football player in the St. Louis region. Ryan was recruited to play football at the University of Missouri. The football career did not work out for him. He returned to St. Charles and continued his studies at Lindenwood University. Ryan began training in boxing part-time as a full-time college student. He had a successful amateur boxing career. Ryan's goal was to become a household name and help others see that second chances and second careers are possible. As a professional, he was invited to be a participant on the TV show *The Contender*. His success on this show caught the attention of legendary boxing promoter Don King. Ryan Coyne has become a top contender in boxing and has a perfect 20-0 record.

I enjoyed meeting Ryan Coyne at a school assembly. He spoke to 500 students about being positive and about not bullying. I asked him about his thoughts on bullies and bullying. His response was, "Bullying comes from insecurity. People bully to make themselves feel better. There's no honor in being a bully. You have to find other ways to make yourself feel better. If you see something like this going on, you need to stick up for the person being bullied. You should always treat someone with the same respect you want to be treated with. Conflicts can be resolved with my most powerful weapon. It isn't my jab or right hook, it's my mind."

Kim Vandenberg (Olympic Swimmer)

Kim Vandenberg

Kim Vandenberg was born in 1983 in Berkeley, California. She swam for Campolindo High School and Orinda Aquatics. Kim swam for and graduated from UCLA. She won a bronze medal in the 2008 Summer Olympics in Beijing. In her free time, Kim enjoys painting, reading, playing piano, photography, and traveling.

She shared her thoughts on bullies, "Unfortunately bullying is very common and has a strong impact of those who are being bullied. My advice would be to seek help from a teacher or a parent. To have an authority figure step in and help mediate the problem can be helpful. Also it's important to remember that often times the person who is doing the bullying is most likely unhappy with themselves in some aspect and therefore releasing their negativity on others. I would recommend not taking offense to the bully and instead try to become friends with this person and find out what their story. Maybe in doing so, a new perspective will appear and both people will end up in a happier place."

CHAPTER 7

Charity, Giving Back & Volunteering

Charity (noun): The voluntary giving of help, typically money, to those in need.

Volunteering (verb): freely offer to do something.

If you can't feed a hundred people, then just feed one.
-Mother Teresa

You give but little when you give of your possessions, it is when you give of yourself that you truly give. -Kahlil Gibran

There is so much more to professional athletes than what is seen on tv and read in magazines. The world's fastest, strongest, best, and most famous do a great deal in their personal lives to better other people's lives. Much of this is done because it is the right thing to do. It is not done for a photo shoot or a PR campaign. A number of the athletes overcame challenges in their own lives. This may have been poverty, a disability, or losing someone close to them. In other cases, the cause may just be something that touched their heart or moved them to act.

Steven Jackson (NFL)

Steven Jackson with Matthew (Compliments of Alvina Alston)

Steven Jackson is a professional football player for the St. Louis Rams. He was drafted in the first round of the 2004 NFL entry draft. Steven is approaching 10,000 career rushing yards and has over 50 rushing touchdowns. In 2010, he became the all-time leading rusher for the St. Louis Rams, breaking Eric Dickerson's record. Steven is known for his speed and strength as a rusher. He is also known for his mental and physical toughness. Steven had his second best rushing year while suffering from major back pains.

Steven has a track record for supporting the communities where he lives and works. He started the SJ39 Foundation in 2004. The foundation supports youth sports programs, cancer research, and education related causes.

When asked about his efforts to give back, he said, "I got started very early in supporting charities. In 2004, I started my foundation. I did this because growing up in Las Vegas we didn't have many sports teams. I didn't grow up having athletes visit my school to tell us to stay in school, work hard, and follow your dreams. So I wanted to do this in Las Vegas and also here in St. Louis. I enjoy it and the kids enjoy it. I could see in the kids' faces that this was really special for them."

Gerry Cooney (Retired Pro Boxer)

Gerry Cooney was born in Long Island, NY in the 1950's. He was a very successful amateur boxer who won many tournaments all over the world. Gerry stood at 6'6" and is a southpaw (lefty). This made him a very tough match-up for other fighters in his division. As a professional boxer, his career record was 28-3. Gerry's biggest win came against former world champion Ken Norton. His only losses came to three of the best boxers of all time - Larry Holmes, Michael Spinks, and George Foreman.

Gerry Cooney is very committed to helping others. He supports his community in many ways. One example he shared was, "I go to an orphanage twice a week. I teach the kids boxing, but more importantly, I teach them life skills. If you can learn to fight, you can learn to do anything. You also need to follow your dream."

Leila Hurst (Pro Surfer)

Leila Hurst was born on the Island of Kauai, Hawaii in 1993. She started surfing at just three years old. Leila was sponsored by Billabong at nine and was first featured in a sports magazine at the age of 11. She is currently the only female sponsored by apparel company Vans. Leila has won many tournaments and has been recognized for her accomplishments.

I asked Leila about what she likes to do in her free time. Her answer was, "I love to help out organizations such as Life Rolls On. It is a foundation that take disabled people surfing."

Cam Janssen (NHL)

Cam Janssen

One of the toughest players in the NHL is Cam Janssen. He was born in Eureka, MO, a suburb of St. Louis. Cam's NHL statistics are quite impressive. In just over 300 games, he has over 700 penalty minutes. His role is to make sure the other team is playing "honest" and not taking cheap shots against their star players. Cam is barely six feet tall and almost 200 pounds. Most other enforcers are several inches taller and weigh about 20-30 pounds more than Cam. He definitely holds his own with these guys. When not playing hockey, he trains in mixed martial arts.

Cam is very patriotic and supports those who fight to keep our country free. He told me, "I work with Fisher House. They built this house for families of loved ones who were injured during war. It is a beautiful house that overlooks the Mississippi River - down by Jefferson Barracks. The families can be together when they are in the hospital next door. It is a great thing for those people that have served and fought for our country."

CHAPTER 8

Following Your Dream

Dream (noun): a series of thoughts, images, and sensations occurring in a person's mind during sleep.

All our dreams can come true, if we have the courage to pursue them.
-Walt Disney

Every great dream begins with a dreamer. Always remember, you have within you the strength, the patience, and the passion to reach for the stars to change the world. -Harriet Tubman

During the athlete interviews, it was so interesting to hear that they all had a dream about being a successful athlete. This dream started when they were young. The athletes had the dream, the passion, and the persistence to make it to the top. These messages inspired me to keep following my dream of being a sports reporter.

Nastia Liukin (Olympic Gymnast)

Nastia Liukin (USA Gymnastics – John Cheng)

Nastia Liukin was born in Moscow, Russia in 1989. She moved to the United States when she was two years old. Nastia's parents, Valeri and Anna, were both accomplished gymnasts. Her father won a gold and silver medal at the 1988 Olympic games. He serves as Nastia's gymnastics coach.

Nastia began showing talent in gymnastics at the young age of three. Her success continued throughout her youth and into her teens. Nastia qualified for the 2008 Olympics in Beijing. She won five medals - all around gold medal, three silver medals and a bronze medal. Nastia's performance at the Olympics helped her to achieve international recognition. She has appeared in several television shows and commercials.

Nastia believes very strongly in goal setting, hard work and dreaming big, "Never be afraid to dream too big. Set daily, weekly, monthly and yearly goals for yourself and never give up on them. When you finally achieve them nothing can compare to that feeling."

Mario Chalmers (NBA)

Mario Chalmers was born in Anchorage, Alaska in 1986. Alaska is not usually thought of as the birthplace of a professional basketball player. Mario attended Bartlett High School. He was named State Player of the Year three times in a row. Mario led his high school to two state championships.

Mario was the #2 rated point guard in the nation in the 2005 recruiting class. He committed to play for the University of Kansas. In college, Mario was very successful - earning a most outstanding player in the NCAA tournament. He helped Kansas to win the National Championship in 2008. This performance led to him being drafted into the NBA. He currently plays for the Miami Heat.

When I asked Mario about his favorite part about being an NBA player, he answered, "My favorite part is that it fulfilled my dream of becoming an NBA player. A dream I had since I was a little kid."

Alex Pietrangelo (NHL)

Alex Pietrangelo (credit – St. Louis Blues)

Alex Pietrangelo is one of the best young defenseman in the National Hockey League. He plays for the St. Louis Blues. Alex was drafted fourth overall in the 2008 NHL entry draft. In 2011-2012, he finished in the top five among defenseman in scoring with 51 points.

Alex talked about pursuing his dream as a pro hockey player, "The best part of being a pro hockey player is probably the fact that I get to do what I love and make a living from it. Growing up I always wanted to be a professional hockey player which is probably similar to every person in pro hockey. I feel privileged to be able to still be playing it (hockey) as often as I do."

Kristy Kowal (Olympic Swimmer & Elementary School Teacher)

Kristy Kowal won the silver medal in the 200 meter breaststroke at the 2000 Summer Olympics in Sydney, Australia. She graduated from the University of Georgia in 2002 with a Bachelor of Science degree in Education. Kristy is now an elementary school teacher in Pennsylvania.

Kristy shared her experience and advice about following dreams, "I am a big advocate of following your dream. I wanted to make the Olympic swimming team when I was 8 years old. Mind you I could barely make a full lap of swimming without stopping. But no one ever told me that I couldn't do it. My parents told me that if that is what I wanted to do then I should never give up on that. I also think setting goals is extremely important, whether in sports or in life. Goals help you focus on what you want to achieve and once you have your goal you can start coming up with a plan to reach your goal. I think it is important to have short term and long term goals. The Olympics is only every 4 years. So if the only goal I ever had was the make the Olympics, I think I would have driven myself crazy just focusing on that. So I took everything year by year, thinking about times I wanted to go, teams I wanted to make that would help me achieve the long term goal of the Olympics. I think when you make a goal and say it out loud, it becomes more concrete."

Jim Craig (Hockey - "Miracle on Ice" Goalie)

Jim Craig was born in Easton, Massachusetts in 1957. He attended Boston University and helped lead the team to the NCAA Division I championship in 1978. Jim was named an NCAA All-Star in 1979.

Jim is best known as the goalie for the 1980 US Olympic hockey team. The team was a heavy underdog going into the Olympics. In the game against the Soviets, the Americans were outshot 42-16, but Jim made 39 saves, many of the spectacular variety, and his teammates scored four times. The US team won that game 4-3. Two days later they beat Finland and clinched the Olympic gold medal for the US. The team was later referred to as the "Miracle on Ice". The story became a very successful movie - *Miracle*. I asked Jim about his thoughts about the team success and about the movie:

"It was part of our legacy, something that we are very proud of and that a lot of people made a lot of personal sacrifices so we could achieve."

Jim Craig went on to play pro hockey until his retirement from hockey in 1984. After his hockey career, Jim became involved in motivational speaking and marketing. He is the president of Gold Medal Strategies, a Boston-based promotions and marketing firm.

Jim shared his advice for aspiring pro hockey players on how to achieve their dream, "I would tell any hockey player to believe in a dream and make all the personal sacrifices they need to so that they have no regrets."

CHAPTER 9

More Great Advice

I have learned so many important lessons over the past two years from some incredible athletes, who are also incredible people. There were far too many items to fit in the previous chapters, so you will find some highlights in this chapter. My hope is that this book is only the beginning of my journey. I plan to continue interviewing athletes and sharing what I learn with others. This is my way of paying this experience forward. The best news I could get is to learn that other kids are inspired to follow their dreams too.

Agnes Zawadzki (Olympic Figure Skater)

Having a positive attitude helps you train at a higher level because you won't get frustrated easily, which can hinder a practice session. When you have an open mind, you're willing to try new things to get better as an athlete and you're willing to work hard on getting a new skill.

Anastasia Ashley (Surfer)

Very important, I think being an athlete, and especially becoming a professional athlete takes sometimes many years of dedication, long hours, blood, sweat, and tears. There's a lot that goes into as well as from the mental standpoint of being able to perform under pressure, and perform under high stressed situations which also can apply to other aspects of your life.

Bradley Beal (Basketball Player)

Any good mental state of mind will help you do anything you want to because it makes you believe you can do it. Hard work is very important. The more practice the better you are. This is especially true in transitioning from high school to college ball. I'm not the only great player on the court anymore.

Brigetta Barrett (Track & Field)

The only thing you truly have control over is your attitude. You may wake up sick the morning of a major competition, it may be pouring rain during the Super bowl but if the competition is not delayed, you still have to compete. And the only thing that is going to get you through sickness, bad weather, or any trial that threatens your success is a positive attitude.

Brittney Lincicome (LPGA Golfer)

In golf, honesty and integrity play a large role. You are responsible for calling penalties on yourself if you make a mistake, and I love the honor in seeing a player do so.

Cassie Gannis (Professional Race Car Driver)

I'm a firm believer in working to make your dream happen. In school I found that my struggles with reading were because of dyslexia, and then in 2006, I needed to take 8 months off for spinal surgery. Learning to work through these challenges has taught me about perseverance and motivation. Always keep your goals in mind. It's amazing what will happen. Overcoming both those challenges has been among my proudest moments.

Chellsie Memmel (Olympic Gymnast)

Work hard and always have goals set so you have something to work towards.

Chipper Jones (MLB)

Work hard in the classroom and on the field. Both of those are equally important to succeed in life. Without one, the other doesn't exist.

Dana Hee (Olympic Gold Medalist – Tae Kwon Do)

Follow your dream! Set and prioritize little goals then follow them step by step. Never take your eye off each tiny step!!! And NEVER give up. When met with obstacles...find a way around them!

Danielle Pascente (Fitness Model)

To be successful in anything you have to first be honest with yourself and secondly maintain that integrity in your follow through. Honesty is always the best policy. Having a pure heart shows on and off the field, in and out of the office. You may be a star player, but if you cannot conduct yourself with class, people may look at you differently. Integrity is that extra component that makes you stand out in a crowd of people. If you can respect yourself and be honest with others... that will translate in everything you do.

Doug Flutie (Retired Football Player)

I think the advice is that believing in yourself is what is the most impor-tant. Obviously, I've faced challenges in my career where I was written off many times and people didn't believe I had what it took to succeed on the pro level. But what they thought didn't matter- I believed in myself and I worked my tail off to become successful.

Emily Hughes (Olympic Figure Skater)

Hard work is one of the most important things in sports. The other is having fun. Without working hard, and enjoying the sport, I would not have made the Olympic team. I always found that when I worked hard and felt prepared for a competition, I always did better than I expected.

Fred Lynn (Retired MLB)

The best leaders lead by example not by what they tell you. They go out and do all the right things.

Jack Clark (Retired MLB)

Respect the game. Nobody is bigger than the game. It is about the name on the front of the jersey more than the name on the back. Play as hard as you can for as long as you can. Make them have to tear the uniform off of you. Don't cheat. Be true to yourself. Work hard in the off-season. It is a short career – so go to school and get a good education. You never want to forget that you were a lucky one for making it.

Jen Welter (Pro Football)

Never let anyone limit your dreams or your drive. No one should be able to deter you from dreaming big and working to accomplish your dreams.

Jim Fox (NHL Player & Broadcaster)

This goes back to being honest with yourself, only you know how hard you are working and how hard you can work. You need to work hard and you need to work and rest smart. I know of no one that became successful without a strong work ethic.

JP Arencibia (MLB)

Always concentrate on school. Baseball can be taken away from you at any-time. You always want to have something to fall back on. Also, always out-work the guy next to you. Try to be the hardest worker out there - the first one there and the last one to leave.

Kristina Thorson (Softball)

My whole life, all my coaches have tried to tell me that I'm too small, too short, don't throw hard enough, or just plain wasn't good enough to be an elite pitcher. Even into my professional career I still face those naysayers. While it was always a difficult situation, because I didn't get much pitching time, I think that was also the best situation for me in the end because of the motivation it provided me and the work ethic it instilled in me.

Laura Wilkinson (Olympic Diver)

There will be easy days and tough days. If you can push through and work extra hard on the tough days, you'll be amazed at what you can do when you don't feel 100%; then just imagine what you can do when you feel your best! Also, never give up. I know it sounds cliché', but it's truly not over til it's over.

Louis Coleman (MLB Player)

I think that the work and effort that a person puts into baseball is very comparable to the attitude that someone should have in life. A baseball player can't just sneak by with mediocrity just as a lawyer couldn't afford to not be prepared for a trial. You have to have a drive in you that makes you want to be the best, just as a business man should too.

Melanie Snare (Cheerleader, Actress, Model)

My advice for anyone pursuing a dream - no matter what that is - would be to do your research, prepare yourself in any way that you need to do so (dance classes, acting classes, photo shoots, gain experience, etc) and never give up! With cheerleading, acting, modeling - in the world that I live - rejection is part of the game. But you can't take no for an answer. You have to learn from it, keep working hard and try again. Always chase your dreams but know that with that needs to come dedication, a strong work ethic and perseverance!

Phil Bourque (Retired NHL Player & Broadcaster)

Having a positive attitude and a true love for what you do will help you through the negative road blocks that are bound to come your way as an athlete.

Phil Housley (Retired NHL Player)

It takes a tremendous amount of commitment when you decide what you want to do. However, if you love what you do and you have passion doing it, you can make a difference!

Scott Norton (NHL Agent)

Author Matthew Pearlman with Sports Agent Scott Norton

We have to be true to ourselves first and foremost. You will never be a winner if you don't have honesty, integrity, and a positive attitude. They play a big part in who you are as a person.

Sinjin Smith (Pro Volleyball Player)

Success in sports and life doesn't come easy. If you ask anyone who has had success what they did to get there, they will always tell you it was through putting in the time and energy that eventually lead to success. No great person was great without working hard. There may be those who have raw talent that have limited success but those who end up doing consistently well have prepared properly and can perform consistently at the highest level. You will always play the way you practice.

Wiley Petersen (Pro Bull Rider)

Work hard, set goals, and do it because you love it. You have to work at it every day.

CHAPTER 10

List of Athletes Featured in the Book

The following athletes are featured in the book, sorted by sport.

BASEBALL:

- JP Arencibia
- Jack Clark
- Louis Coleman
- Andre Dawson
- Rich "Goose" Gossage
- Cole Hamels
- Chipper Jones
- Fred Lynn
- Randy Wells

BASKETBALL:

- Bradley Beal
- Mario Chalmers
- Kevin "Special K" Daley
- Kevin Durant

BILLIARDS:

- Jennifer Barretta

BOWLING:

- Linda Norry Barnes

BOXING:

- Gerry Cooney
- Ryan Coyne
- Amy Hayes

CHEERLEADING:

- Megan LaTempt
- Melanie Snare

FITNESS MODEL:

- Danielle Pascente

FOOTBALL:

- Chase Coffman
- Daniel Fells
- Doug Flutie
- Steven Jackson
- Haloti Ngata
- Jen Welter
- George Wilson

GOLF:

- Brittany Lincicome
- Ryan Palmer

HOCKEY:

- Phil Bourque
- Dustin Brown
- Jim Craig
- Jim Fox
- Phil Housley
- Brett Hull

- Cam Janssen
- Jim Kyte
- Bernie Nicholls
- Alex Pietrangelo
- Keith Tkachuk

MMA:

- Sarah Kaufman
- Mark Munoz
- Brittney Palmer
- Tyron Woodley

NASCAR:

- Kyle Busch
- Cassie Gannis
- David Gilliland
- Juan Pablo Montoya

OLYMPICS:

- Brigetta Barrett
- Usain Bolt
- Alissa Czisny
- Devon Harris
- Dana Hee
- Emily Hughes
- Jill Kintner
- Nastia Liukin
- Kristy Kowal
- Chellsie Memmel
- Consuella "Connie" Moore
- Nikki Stone
- Kim Vandenberg
- Jennifer Wester
- Laura Wilkinson
- Agnes Zawadzki

PRO BULL RIDER:

- Wiley Petersen

SOCCER:

- Nicole Barnhart
- Peter Lowry

SOFTBALL:

- Kristina Thorson

SPORTS AGENT:

- Scott Norton

SURFER:

- Anastasia Ashley
- Leila Hurst

TENNIS:

- Shahar Pe'er

VOLLEYBALL:

- Sinjin Smith

WRESTLER - PROFESSIONAL:

- Jessie Godderz

CHAPTER 11

Athletes Thoughts About the Book

Agnes Zawadzki (Olympic – Skater)

This would have been a type of book that I would have read because it seems like it would be really helpful to me as an athlete. The title would have grabbed my attention for sure. These lessons can also apply to life, not just sports.

Alissa Czisny (Olympic Skater)

Your book sounds great; what a wonderful idea for young students! I definitely would have read that type of book as a student. Even now, I like to read those types of books, both for motivation and inspiration, as well as to work on improving my own character.

Bernie Nicholls (Retired NHL Player)

Absolutely, this is a book I would have read. A lot of people don't understand how you need to work hard and something like this would be perfect for kids to read. People of all ages can always learn from stuff like this.

Brett Hull (Former NHL Player)

I definitely would have read this book as a kid. Any time you can help young people deal with tough problems, it is very important. The stories and advice from successful people that have already dealt with these issues and overcome them will help others.

Cole Hamels (MLB Player)

I think this book will help students to know what it takes to get to the top and how to stay there. Of course this would have been a book that I would have read as a student.

Daniel Fells (NFL Player)

I think this is an excellent idea. I often go to schools and speak to kids on topics like this, and I often times think about what kind of effect it would have had on me at that age. I think it would have been a positive one.

David Gilliland (NASCAR)

The biggest thing kids can learn is that great athletes at the top of their game are just normal people. They do have extreme dedication to their sport and they practice a lot. It can help kids to read about athletes and true stories about decisions they made and why.

Dustin Brown (NHL Player)

This book is great for students. I wish there had been something like this for me to read growing up. There are books I read today that I find interest in because the same core thoughts are being discussed. As much as I have learned about leadership there is still much I don't know and knowledge is power.

Doug Flutie (Retired Pro Football Player)

I think that this is a great book. Many kids look up to sports stars and that is great, if the sports stars are good role models for the kids, which the athletes you are interviewing for this book seem to be. I would definitely have read this book when I was growing up. Hearing inspirational words from your favorite athletes is always a good thing.

Emily Hughes (Olympic Skater)

I always enjoyed reading books about people who accomplished things through hard work and determination. I also love reading about people who help other people and make the world a better place. The book you are putting together sounds like it would be very inspirational to anyone reading it.

Fred Lynn (Retired MLB Player)

I think a lot of guys will read this kind of book. When I was 13-14 years old, I was reading a lot of books about athletes. I think kids your age would love to read what athletes have to say.

George Wilson (NFL Player)

I would've enjoyed reading it as a young kid because of the insight it gives you. You are addressing a variety of issues that young kids have to go through each and every day. They have to endure those battles and sometimes you have to go through those negative experiences to realize the lesson that's to be learned. So if you can gain it through reading the book then it can save you some headache and heartache.

Haloti Ngata (NFL Player)

I think this book is awesome. A lot of kids out there need something like this so they can see that not everyone is perfect. Everybody faces trials and tribulations in trying to get where they are. It's also great because there are kids, who at a young age have all the talent and God-given ability, but then they face an obstacle and they give up. They might think everything should come easily, but it doesn't. Definitely, my mom would have found this book and have had me read it. My mom was always trying to find me books so I could read something positive or something I could learn from. I definitely would have benefited from a book like this. (Note: Haloti's mother and father both died while he was in college. That was the challenge he overcame).

Jessie Godderz (Professional Wrestler & Reality TV Star)

I think that book is an absolutely brilliant idea. It's definitely the type of book I would have read growing up...and would definitely still read now! In sports and in the rest of life, as long as you work hard, never give up, treat your teammates with the utmost respect, and go after your goals no matter what hardships stand in your way, you've got the best chance of achieving your dreams. You CAN realize your dreams. I'm living proof, and I couldn't be more happy or fulfilled with my choices.

Jill Kintner (Olympic Skier)

I love to read inspiring stories, but it's just as important to create your own stories. Inspiration comes from everywhere. Anything that inspires or motivates someone is good.

Juan Pablo Montoya (NASCAR)

The important thing for me is that even if one word of my experience or thoughts helps someone then doing something like this is more than worth it. I think it's a great way to reach people and I'm happy to be a part of this book.

Keith Tkachuk (Retired NHL Player)

 I think it is a good concept. Having two boys 12 and 14, it is hard to find books that are interesting and they can relate to.

Kevin "Special K" Daley (Harlem Globetrotters)

Definitely, this is a wonderful idea. I'm really happy that you're getting all the support from these athletes. This shows that athletes do care about kids. It's even more special because it's coming from another kid. I'm glad I am able to help with it, and I can't wait to read it myself! My daughter is 6 and she's reading now, so I am going to pass it to her.

Linda Norry Barnes (Professional Bowler)

Reading a book with Lessons from the World's Greatest Athletes is like getting a head start in life. We can always learn from others, and the people that are competing daily are the best examples you can have on what to do and sometimes what not to do. I personally love to read about people and their life experiences. I can always find something that relates to my life and learn some new lessons on what to do better in the future.

Louis Coleman (MLB Player)

I think the idea for a book like this is pretty cool. It is another way to give young kids a perspective of a professional athlete, but this time from another kid's point of view. It is also another way to help kids aspire to be something in life and to set goals.

Mark Munoz (MMA Fighter)

I love these kinds of books! There needs to be a resurgence of character, integrity, and leadership in our young people today. I would definitely read a book like this.

Megan LaTempt (NFL Cheerleader)

As a teacher, I feel this is a great book idea for students! Hopefully by reading this book it will inspire young adults to join an organization and think about career choices. Also, it will be beneficial for students to see what character items are important and must be present in order to have a successful organization. Yes, I would have loved to have been given the opportunity to read a book such as this because it would have been wonderful to see a peer as the author and would have been very inspirational to me!

Nicole Barnhart (Pro Soccer Player)

Sometimes we forget to step back and listen to what others have to say and look at what others can teach us through their experiences. This is definitely a book I would have read as a student, and would still read today.

Nikki Stone (Olympic Freestyle Skier)

All my greatest lessons I learned through sports and my sports heroes. I think a book like this can help students learn the most important characteristics of being a successful human being who is both productive and giving.

Peter Lowry (Pro Soccer Player)

Growing up, I read a few motivational books. I remember one by Summer Sanders that really was a great book about positive thinking and setting goals. Your book can be a great tool for people who can look at what professional athlete's value and learn a few tools to help them achieve their own goals. I really commend you for writing this and hope it can help inspire people to achieve greatness.

Phil Housley (Former NHL player)

This book would have been a great read to have growing up, especially coming from ordinary people who have done amazing things in sports. There is a reason why people in life or sports are successful, and to hear their advice would be beneficial to find out what made them successful!

Scott Norton (Sports Agent)

I think this is a great idea, and I think students need to learn and understand what it really takes to make it in sports. What a great way to learn these things as they are learning them from the best!   100%! I was and always have been a sports junkie so a book like this about athletes and teaching me to be a better athlete would have been #1 on my bookshelf.

Sinjin Smith (Retired Pro Volleyball Player)

In life, experience is critical, but knowledge is even more important. The more information we can get from those who have come before us and who have gone through the experiences we will end up going through, the better chance we will have in not making some of their mistakes. We progress as a society and individually by learning from those who came before us.

About the Author

Matthew Pearlman is a 13 year old middle school student who lives in St. Louis, MO. He has a passion for sports. Matthew enjoys playing several sports including – hockey, basketball, and he trains in martial arts. At school, Matthew serves as a mentor tutor for second graders, volunteering 20 hours per month with at-risk students. When he is not at school, volunteering, or playing sports, he spends his time writing sports articles, researching about sports, interviewing athletes, and attending sporting events. He has been a credentialed media member at several national and regional sporting events. Matthew's knowledge of sports, athletes, and statistics, helps him to hold his own with veteran reporters. He has a twin sister, Samantha, who is a middle school cheerleader. She is often the person he bounces ideas off of. Matthew would like to be either a sports agent or sports broadcaster when he grows up.

CPSIA information can be obtained at www.ICGtesting.com
Printed in the USA
LVOW122137050712

288970LV00007B/44/P